THE STORY OF

DANIEL BOONE,

WILDERNESS EXPLORER

THE STORY OF

DANIEL BOONE, Wilderness Explorer

BY WALTER RETAN

COVER ILLUSTRATION BY MARIE DEJOHN
INTERIOR ILLUSTRATIONS BY STEVEN PETRUCCIO

A YEARLING BOOK

ABOUT THIS BOOK

The events described in this book are true. They have been carefully researched and excerpted from authentic autobiographies, writings, and commentaries. No part of this biography has been fictionalized.

To learn more about Daniel Boone, ask your librarian to recommend other fine books you might read.

Published by
Dell Publishing
a division of
Bantam Doubleday Dell Publishing Group, Inc.
1540 Broadway
New York, New York 10036

ISBN: 0-440-40711-7

Published by arrangement with Parachute Press, Inc.
Printed in the United States of America
October 1992
10 9 8 7 6 5
OPM

To Kathy and Betsy

Contents

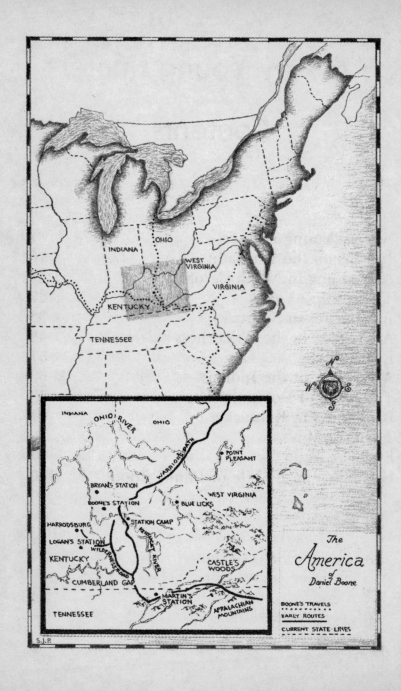

The
America
of
Daniel Boone

BOONE'S TRAVELS
EARLY ROUTES
CURRENT STATE LINES

A Very Young Hunter

From the time he was a young boy living on the Pennsylvania frontier, Daniel Boone hated to stay in one place very long. He wanted to be free to wander and explore. When his parents took him to church, his mother had to hold his hand tightly. If she didn't, he would silently slip away. Nobody ever saw him leave. He just vanished.

The only time Daniel was willing to sit quietly and listen was when Indians came to call at the Boone farmhouse. Daniel's father was a weaver and a blacksmith, as well as a farmer. The Indians came to trade furs and animal skins for cloth and metal knives. They squatted outside the stone house to make their trades, speaking English and using Indian hand signs. Usually these Indians were Delaware or Shawnee, who were friendly to the colonists living in Pennsylvania. William Penn, the founder of the colony, had always treated them honestly and well.

Daniel admired the Indians. He knew that they

1

were better than white men at tracking game and finding their way through the thick forests, so he asked them lots of questions. They must have sensed that this small boy appreciated their ways and wanted to learn from them, because they told him their woodland secrets and let him trail through the woods after them. He learned to walk in the forest wilderness without leaving any tracks and to light a fire without using flint or steel. And he became an expert marksman with a bow and arrow.

Daniel was born on November 2, 1734. A few months before his sixth birthday, there was an outbreak of smallpox in the little frontier town where the Boones lived. Many people were dying from the deadly disease, which spread from family to family. Daniel and his brothers and sisters had to stay home. Sarah Boone thought that her children would be safer if she kept them away from other people.

As usual, Daniel couldn't stand being cooped up in the house. He persuaded his older sister Elizabeth to sneak out with him. He thought that if they caught smallpox, they could go wherever they wanted. So Daniel and Elizabeth decided to visit a house where sick people lived.

While the rest of the family slept, the two children crept out of the house. Off they ran to the home of a sick family. There they got into bed with a child who already had smallpox. As soon as they thought they had been there long enough, they ran home and got back into bed. Nobody knew they had been out.

Soon red spots broke out all over their skin. They had both caught the dreaded disease. Sarah Boone wondered how such a thing could have happened. She had been so careful to keep her children at home! Daniel was never good at telling lies. He confessed what he had done. Sarah didn't scold him. She simply said, "Thee naughty boy, why did thee not tell me before so I could have had thee better prepared?"

Sarah Boone probably realized Daniel was born to be outdoors, and the best she could do was try to keep him safe.

Daniel came by his independent spirit very naturally. All of the Boones were an independent lot. Back in England, Grandfather George Boone had left the Church of England to become a Quaker. This was against the law. The king of England had ordered that all Englishmen must worship at the Church of England. But the Quakers—also called the religious Society of Friends—refused to take part in Church of England services. Quakers believed that the relationship between a worshiper and God was private and did not require priests or ministers. They were peaceful people who refused to bear arms or swear oaths. Because large numbers of them

3

were being treated badly and put in prison for their beliefs, many Quakers crossed the ocean to Pennsylvania. William Penn had founded Pennsylvania so that Quakers and other groups could worship in freedom.

Finally George Boone decided that he would go to Pennsylvania too. In 1712, he sent his three eldest children on a ship to Philadelphia. One of them was the sixteen-year-old Squire, who would one day be Daniel's father. Five years later, George made the journey himself, taking the rest of his family with him. He was already fifty-one years old. Few men his age would have had the courage to leave their home for an unknown future.

The Boones eventually settled in a Quaker area on the Schuylkill River, just north of Philadelphia. The land was still quite wild, with stumps and boulders dotting the cleared fields. George bought four hundred acres with the last of his savings. Then he went to work as a weaver and a farmer. His son Squire soon married and settled on a farm next to his father's land. The Boones became important members of the Quaker settlement.

In 1744, when Daniel was ten years old, Squire Boone bought about twenty-five acres of pastureland four miles from the farm. During the late spring and summer, Daniel and his mother took the cattle there to graze. They lived by themselves in a small cabin. While they were gone, Elizabeth Boone looked after the rest of the family.

Daniel loved his freedom as a cowherd. Every morning he drove the cows out to pasture. Then he was free to wander through the woods and hillsides. In the early evening he drove the cows back to the cabin for milking. His mother churned butter and made cheese in a tiny dairy house built over a spring of fresh, cold water. At least once or twice a week one of the other Boone boys came out to visit them and pick up a supply of their mother's fresh butter and cheese. They also brought the latest news from the small village.

While herding cattle, Daniel made his first hunting weapon. He was too young to have a gun. Instead he pulled a young tree out of the ground. Then he shaved the slender trunk until it was smooth, leaving the roots at the bottom. With this simple weapon he could kill a rabbit from ten yards away. He had strong arms and his aim was very accurate.

When Daniel was twelve, his father gave him a rifle. Very quickly the boy became a crack shot. At that time, there were still some wildcats and buffalo in eastern Pennsylvania, and many bears, deer, and beaver lived near the rivers and creeks.

There were also flocks of wild turkeys in the woods. In the fall, when they were at their fattest, Daniel would often shoot one and bring it back to the cabin. He enjoyed cooking a turkey outdoors for his mother. After cleaning and dressing it, he would hang it over a fire by its neck. Then he turned it regularly with a stick so that it roasted evenly without burning. He even basted the turkey, catching the drippings in a piece of curved bark and pouring the juice over the bird. The first time his mother saw this, she asked where he had learned to cook this way. He told her that an Indian had taught him.

Unfortunately, Daniel was far more interested in hunting wild animals than in watching cattle. Cows were too dull for him. Instead of looking after them, he often wandered through the woods and unexplored valleys. He loved to study the behavior of wild birds and animals.

Once, when he was about thirteen, Daniel didn't bring the cows back at the usual time. Sarah had to got after them herself. While she milked them and made butter, she wondered what could have happened to her son. At first she didn't worry too much. She knew Daniel could take care of himself in the wild forest, and he never seemed to get lost.

But morning came and Daniel had still not appeared. Now Sarah *was* worried. She walked to the village to give the alarm. The neighbors immediately organized a search party. For an entire day they searched through the forested valleys and hills, but they found no sign of Daniel. The

next day they traveled even farther away in the direction of the Neversink Mountains. Suddenly in the far distance they spied a cloud of dark smoke rising above the horizon. By the time they reached the smoke, night was falling. In the darkness they discovered a shelter made of bark. Daniel was inside, sitting on a bearskin. A piece of bear meat was roasting on the fire, and the rest of the bear hung nearby.

One of the members of the search party asked Daniel if he was lost. No, he replied. He had been tracking a bear and wanted to get it before he returned to the cabin. Daniel was both pleased and proud. This was the first bear he had ever killed. Now there would be fresh meat for everyone, and he knew that his mother would be happy to have the bear skin.

Daniel's actions made good sense to the men in the search party, who were hunters themselves. And they were glad to eat some of the fresh bear meat that Daniel was roasting over his fire!

By his fifteenth birthday Daniel had already earned a reputation for being the best shot in town. And he was completely at home in the wilderness. Parents never worried about their children if they were out in the woods with Daniel Boone.

Daniel's best friend was a teenager named Henry Miller. Henry, who was three years older than Daniel, worked as an apprentice in Squire

Boone's blacksmith shop. He taught Daniel how to repair rifles and traps. These were two skills that all backwoodsmen needed. The two friends hunted together whenever they could. At least twice they collected enough fur pelts and animal skins to trade for gunpowder and hunting knives in the city of Philadelphia. They also found time to play pranks. Many a neighboring farmer would come out in the morning to find his wagon wheels dangling from the barn roof.

Most of the Boone children spent at least three months of the year in a one-room schoolhouse. But Daniel had little interest in school. He liked arithmetic. Land surveyors used arithmetic, and he thought he might want to become one. But as for spelling—why would a hunter need to know that? His mother seemed to understand and didn't insist that he go. As a result, Daniel didn't learn to read and write until he was almost fourteen years old. He might never have learned if his older brother's wife hadn't taught him herself, but he was always a poor speller.

Daniel had his own special place in the Boone family—as hunter, explorer, and pathfinder. His great love of nature and adventure would one day play a very important part in the growth of the United States.

Indians on the Warpath

In 1750, the Boones decided to move. A few years earlier, Daniel's oldest sister, Sarah, had married a man who was not a Quaker. The Society of Friends expelled her from the group, forcing her father to apologize for her behavior. Five years later, Daniel's oldest brother, Israel, also married out of the Quaker faith. He, too, was expelled. But this time Squire Boone refused to apologize. He believed his children should be free to marry anyone they wanted. The Friends were outraged by his independence and proceeded to expel *him* as well.

Years earlier Grandfather Boone had left the Church of England because he wanted to be free to worship as a Quaker. Now his son was leaving the Quakers because he felt that they had become just as narrow-minded as the church they had left in England. He also believed that too many settlers were crowding into Pennsylvania. They were buying all the land and killing the game. He longed to see wild forests again. So Squire Boone sold his land, his home, and everything that was too big to load into a wagon and headed south to North Carolina. He had heard there was plenty of rich land down there, just waiting to be claimed.

On the morning of May 1, everyone gathered to leave. Two of Daniel's cousins, as well as his friend Henry Miller, were going along. They piled their belongings into a few covered wagons and set off with some horses and a herd of cattle. The children rode in the wagons and the women walked alongside. The older boys brought up the rear, prodding the cattle now and then to make sure they didn't stray. Daniel walked with the men at the head of the wagon train. He was almost sixteen now, and he carried his long rifle in his arms. His keen blue eyes were on the alert, watching for game or unfriendly Indians.

For many days the wagons bounced along, passing between dark mountains and thick forests. (From time to time the party stopped to camp overnight, then packed up to continue the long journey.) As the little group passed through the great Shenandoah Valley into Virginia, they came upon a settlement where they found old friends from Pennsylvania. So the Boones decided to unpack and stay for a while. Squire set up shop as a blacksmith.

Daniel and Henry, however, were not ready to

stop so soon. They wanted to scout the North Carolina countryside. Traveling south, all the way to the Yadkin River valley, they caught so much game that they had a whole load of furs and animal skins. They decided to return to Philadelphia to sell them—and made thirteen hundred dollars! Unfortunately, they spent most of the money on having a good time. When they returned to the family, they had nothing left but the gifts they brought back. All his life Daniel would have trouble managing his money.

But Daniel had also brought back something precious—exciting stories about the Yadkin Valley. He told his family about the rich soil that was completely free of the big rocks that had been such a nuisance in Pennsylvania. Cold, clear streams flowed down the woodsy mountainsides to nourish the soil, and tall canebrakes covered the lowlands. These great clusters of reeds sometimes grew sixteen feet high! The countryside was filled with game. And there were few settlers to hunt it.

Squire Boone listened to the glowing tales and decided the time had come to move on. During their first winter in North Carolina, they had to live in a cave. But when spring came, they built a rough log cabin. Squire worked as a blacksmith and did enough farming to provide fresh vegetables for the family. Daniel helped with the farming, but he could scarcely wait for winter. Then he would be free to roam the countryside hunting game.

As a hunter, Daniel was a great success. He took off into the forests with a packhorse or two and his trusty rifle. But he always returned with a heap of deer skins and beaver, and otter furs. The skin of a buck—a male deer—was especially valuable, because it could be made into a pair of men's pants. One buckskin sold for a dollar. This is why people started to call a dollar a "buck."

Daniel was a frequent visitor at the market town of Salisbury, North Carolina, where he brought his catch to trade for goods. One day he arrived in Salisbury with a load of furs from his traps. Two men took one look at him and decided he must be some simple country boy. They came up with a plan to cheat him, challenging him to a shooting match. Daniel immediately took them up on their bet.

First they gave him a few easy targets and let him win. Then one of the men said, "I'll bet you a hundred dollars against your furs on one more shot." Daniel accepted their offer. The man nailed a paper target to the tree. Daniel didn't notice that the target was already pierced with a bullet hole—right next to the bull's-eye. But he did notice that when the man shot, he swerved his gun so far to one side that the bullet couldn't possibly have gone near the target. Daniel realized right away that he had been taken for a fool, but he didn't let on. Instead he congratulated the man, then prepared for his own shot. Taking careful aim, he fired—straight through the bull's-eye!

In North Carolina, Daniel met his first unfriendly Indians. The nearby Catawba tribe was on peaceful terms with the white settlers, but fierce parties of Shawnee and Cherokee began to make sudden surprise raids on some of the frontier farms. There were many reasons for the Indians' hostility. Perhaps the most important was the ever-increasing number of people coming to the New World from Europe. By now more than a million and a half white settlers lived in the thirteen colonies along the Atlantic seacoast. As the cities and towns became more and more crowded, the settlers started moving west toward the Appalachian Mountains. They were cutting down trees and killing game in lands where Indians had lived for a long time.

The powerful Iroquois tribe had always lived to the northeast. Now the new settlements were pushing them west and south into Shawnee territory. This forced the Shawnee to move farther south, where they ran into problems with the Cherokee. The powerful Cherokee felt the Kentucky territory, west of the Catawba's land, was theirs.

France was also responsible for stirring up the

Indians. The French claimed the land along the Mississippi River and north into Canada, but the French did not establish colonies the way the English did. Instead they sent trappers and hunters to bring back valuable animal furs and skins. These trappers mingled with the Indians, often living with a tribe for long periods. They didn't bring wives or build houses. And they didn't cut down trees and plow fields for farming.

Because there were only seventy to eighty thousand French people living in America, the French became alarmed. If the English colonists kept moving westward, they would soon be spilling over into French territory. The French began to frighten the Indians with tales of how the English would take away their lands. They urged them to fight the colonists if they wanted to keep their hunting grounds to themselves.

The English decided to move more people into the area to protect their land from the French. They wanted to settle a colony of about three hundred settlers in the fertile valley along the Ohio River. A young American officer named George Washington was sent to a French fort on the southern shore of Lake Erie. He had been told to warn the French to get out of the area before they were driven out. When the French made it clear that they intended to stay, Washington—with about 150 men—built a fort at the place where the Allegheny and Monongahela rivers flowed into the Ohio River. (This is where Pittsburgh is today.)

Washington had not had much experience as a soldier. He picked a poor site for the fort. The Indians and French were able to fire down on his men from surrounding hills, forcing Washington to retreat. The French then built their own fort in the Ohio River valley. They called it Fort Duquesne.

In February 1755, a British general, Edward Braddock, arrived in Virginia. He brought with him two regiments of experienced British infantrymen. Their mission was to drive the French out of Fort Duquesne. Braddock spent several months gathering supplies. He had no idea of what it would be like to fight Indians in the wilderness. Instead of taking packhorses, he insisted on a great wagon train to haul food supplies, cannons, and ammunition.

In addition to his well-trained regulars, the general had a force of colonial militiamen. Among them was Daniel Boone, a wagon driver and blacksmith for the militia. The leader of the militiamen was George Washington, who served as an aide to General Braddock. Washington tried to convince Braddock that he had to fight the Indians in their own way, but Braddock wouldn't listen. He marched his men off into the woods in their bright red coats and wide white shoulder belts. Because there was no road wide enough for the wagons once they got out of Virginia, the militiamen were put to work chopping down trees and hacking a way through the wilderness. The work took so long and was so noisy that the general might as well have sent a messenger telling the French he was on the way.

One of the wagon drivers who accompanied Daniel was a trader named John Findley. They became good friends. At night around the campfire Findley told colorful tales about a territory called Kentucky. The Iroquois called the land *Ken-ta-ke,* which meant "place of fields." In Kentucky the streams were full of fish. The air was crowded with ducks and geese, and buffalo and deer roamed the land. Daniel was fascinated by Findley's stories. And there was plenty of time to talk, because the trip was taking forever. The weary men began to call the Allegheny Mountains the Endless Mountains.

On the morning of July 9, 1755, the British finally crossed the Monongahela River. They were twelve miles from Fort Duquesne. Suddenly a terrifying blast of rifle fire burst out of the thick forest brush on either side of them. It was coming from Potawatomi and Ottawa tribesmen hidden among the trees. Up ahead a force of French soldiers blocked the road. Braddock foolishly tried to keep his men in neat organized rows. But this made the British a perfect target. As the gunfire became heavier, the men panicked. They had never had any experience fighting an enemy they couldn't see. The redcoats broke their lines, turned, and ran.

Washington begged permission to take his militiamen into the woods to fight the Indians in their own way. Braddock refused. Instead he tried desperately to reorganize his troops. Four horses were shot out from under him while he rode back and forth. Finally Braddock himself was hit—by a fatal bullet through his lungs. Under the command of Washington, the survivors began to retreat.

At first the wagon drivers tried to hold out. But soon the Indians began to close in. Daniel and his fellow drivers quickly cut the harnesses from the horses and galloped away. The first campaign in the French and Indian War had been a disaster.

By the end of the summer Daniel Boone was back home in North Carolina.

A Wedding in North Carolina

On the long trail back to North Carolina, Daniel may have been thinking that it was time to marry and settle down. About a year earlier, his sister Mary had married a young neighbor named William Bryan. At the wedding Daniel had met William's younger sister, Rebecca. She must have made a lasting impression. Soon after Daniel returned to the Yadkin Valley, he started calling on her. She was a tall, dark, attractive young woman who seemed completely at home on the frontier.

Daniel was shy around women, but this never stopped him from going after what he wanted. He liked Rebecca's frank way of talking and her honesty. One day they went on a cherry-picking picnic. While they ate lunch on the grass, Daniel got out his hunting knife and began tossing it around. Suddenly it slipped out of his hand. The sharp blade went through Rebecca's white cambric apron. Cambric aprons—aprons made of

very fine linen—were hard to get on the frontier. Most young women would have been very upset to have a young man carelessly tear a hole in such fine cloth. Rebecca simply told Daniel not to worry about it and went right on with their conversation.

Years later, Daniel claimed that he had done it on purpose. He wanted to test Rebecca's temper and to see if she cared about fine clothes. When he saw how unconcerned she was, he knew at once that she would make a good frontier wife.

Rebecca liked the serious, quiet-spoken young man, and both families approved of the match. Rebecca was only seventeen years old and Daniel was just twenty-one.

In those days the future groom had to bring the carcass of a deer to the home of his bride-to-be. That was no problem for Daniel. He not only brought a deer but also cleaned it and cut up the meat as well. Rebecca's whole family gathered around to watch him work. Her parents didn't have to worry about Daniel's ability to provide plenty of game for his family!

Squire Boone was now serving as a justice of the peace on the North Carolina border. There was still no church in the small frontier settlement, so he married the young couple himself. Rebecca arrived at the ceremony riding on her father's horse. When she left, she and her husband were both riding on *his* horse.

The Yadkin Valley neighbors celebrated the

21

wedding with a typical backwoods party. They feasted on roasted venison and corn bread, washed down with jugs of corn brew.

Rebecca was a good wife for Daniel. Although she had grown up in a well-off family, she was a simple woman. She had the courage to follow her husband from one wilderness settlement to another and in their fifty-seven years of marriage she seldom complained about the long months she spent alone with her children while Daniel was off hunting.

After a few months, Daniel and Rebecca moved to the Bryan settlement. Daniel worked hard building a cabin, digging a well and clearing some land to plant crops. He never liked farming, but he managed to grow enough to keep his family supplied with vegetables.

In those early frontier days settlers could not rely on farming as their only source of food. They had to have something to eat during the cold winter months. Hunting was what really kept people alive. As a hunter, Daniel excelled. Most men were lucky to trap three or four animals a day, but Daniel often killed as many as thirty. Over a "long hunt"—one that lasted several months—he could make more money than a farmer earned in a whole year. There was a big demand for furs in Europe. All the fashionable men were wearing fur hats, and both men and women had coats trimmed with beaver fur.

Like other frontier women, Rebecca was always busy. She and Daniel eventually had ten children, and she made most of the family clothing. She cooked and cleaned and helped to plant and tend the crops. She was also a very good shot with a musket. She had to be to guard her home and children while Daniel was away. And it wasn't long before Daniel had to leave.

In 1758, there were still problems with the French and Indians. A new general, John Forbes, came from England to lead another attack against Fort Duquesne. Daniel joined up as wagon master with the local militia. This time the British had five times as many men as the French. They also followed a more direct route, building a chain of protective forts as they moved forward. The French commander quickly saw that he was greatly outnumbered. And every day more of his Indian allies were vanishing in the face of the mighty British troops.

Earlier, the British had invited neighboring Indian tribes to a big peace conference. They promised the Indians that settlers would no longer be allowed to move west of the Allegheny Mountains. That was another reason why the Indian warriors were deserting the French. Realizing that his situation was hopeless, the French commander ordered his men to blow up and abandon Fort Duquesne. General Forbes took over the land without even having to fight for it. The English built a new fort there called Fort Pitt.

This time Daniel Boone didn't have to flee to save his life. He could return to North Carolina at his own speed. When he arrived at the cabin, he found that his firstborn son, James, was already walking. A second son, Israel, was in the cradle. Daniel bought 640 acres of land from his father and prepared to settle down to a peaceful life again.

Unfortunately, peace was hard to find in 1758—especially on the North Carolina border. The colonists did not honor the British promises to the Indians. The white settlers kept moving westward, eager for land. It's doubtful if the king of England himself could have stopped them. But the Indians believed the land belonged to them. They had lived and hunted there long before European explorers discovered the new continent. The Indians also couldn't understand the European idea of private property. In Indian culture land existed for the use of the whole tribe. No one individual—and no tribe—owned it. Sometimes tribes fought with each other over hunting rights, but they never fought over ownership. Many colonists, on the other hand, had left Europe just to own a piece of land.

In the spring of 1758, before General Forbes's expedition, a group of Virginians had murdered some Cherokee hunters for no reason at all. Then

24

they killed fourteen more. The families of the victims swore to avenge the deaths. Soon Indian war parties began to swoop down on frontier settlements. They even attacked the county sheriff in his own cabin and killed more than twenty farmers on the upper Yadkin during planting season.

No one was safe. Families slept restlessly in their dark cabins, listening for a messenger's tap on the window. Such a tap was a warning that Indians were approaching. Immediately the whole family would prepare to leave. They picked up what food and clothing they could find in the dark and set out for the nearest fort. Children and adults remained completely silent once they heard the word *Indian*. While walking through the black brush, they peered nervously from side to side, hoping that no Indians were lurking behind the trees.

The Boone family did not escape the threat. Several times they got up in the middle of the night and made the spooky trip to Fort Dobbs. Once his family was safe at the fort, Daniel would go off with the rangers to patrol the mountains and faraway settlements.

Finally the Indians attacked Fort Dobbs itself. The rangers drove away the Cherokee after a fierce battle. But this time Rebecca had had enough of dangerous frontier life. She persuaded Daniel to move the family back to Virginia. His father and mother had already fled to friends in Maryland.

The family packed their belongings into a wagon and headed for Culpeper, Virginia. Daniel's brother Ned and sister Elizabeth and her husband went with them. At Culpeper, Daniel tried to fit into the life of a tobacco-growing community. He worked as a wagon driver again, hauling tobacco to market, but he refused to plant it.

During this time in Virginia, Daniel is supposed to have met George Washington at Fredericksburg. There is no account of what they said to each other. It's hard to imagine the two together: the tall, aristocratic plantation owner and the rough-and-ready frontiersman. If they did meet, no doubt Boone told Colonel Washington that he, too, had served in both the Braddock and Forbes campaigns.

The Restless Years

The next few years were restless, wandering ones for Daniel Boone. He wasn't happy in Culpeper, so soon after the birth of his first daughter, Susannah, in November 1760, he went off on one of his long hunts. This time he headed southwest to the lonely, stony wilderness of eastern Tennessee.

Like other frontiersmen of his time, he wore a long deerskin hunting shirt and a beaver hat. According to legend, he wore a coonskin cap with a tail hanging down his back. But actually he never wore coonskin hats; in fact, he hated them. In the summer he wore a wide-brimmed felt hat. His knife, tomahawk, powder horn, and bullet pouch hung from a belt around his waist and another belt that crossed over his shoulder. At night he tied his moccasins to his rifle, so they would be easy to find if Indians took him by surprise.

After several months in Tennessee, he started back to Virginia. On the way he stopped off in

North Carolina for a visit in the Yadkin Valley. The Cherokee were on the warpath again. He hurried back to Culpeper with his load of furs and skins. Then he returned to North Carolina to join the militia to try to end the Cherokee threat once and for all. The militia fought like the Indians, striking secretly through the forests. Finally they succeeded in driving the Cherokee out of the whole region.

But instead of going back to Virginia, Daniel went to his old farm at Sugartree Creek. He fixed up the cabin they had abandoned and planted a spring crop. Then Daniel went back to Virginia to get his family. He missed them, and thought the time had come to move them back to North Carolina.

Rebecca was relieved—and surprised—to see him. He had been gone so long that she feared he might be dead. There was now another baby girl, Jemima, in the family.

Soon life returned to the deserted Yadkin Valley settlements. The Boone family and many of their former neighbors had returned to open up their abandoned cabins and clear away the overgrown fields.

But Daniel still couldn't settle down. He decided to sell his home and his 640 acres. In February 1764, the family moved again—about sixty-five miles away. The following year they moved two more times. Daniel always seemed to be searching for a less settled place with more game.

About that time the governor of Florida offered one hundred free acres to anyone who would come settle in Florida. Daniel heard about the offer from some of his old militia friends. Immediately he decided that he should go there. His younger brother Squire and six other men joined the expedition. They left in August 1765, promising their families that they would be home for Christmas dinner.

The five-hundred-mile hike south to the Gulf of Mexico proved to be a near disaster. The men had to tramp through swamps full of mosquitoes and other insects, and there was very little game to kill for food. They might have starved to death if Daniel hadn't made friends with the local Seminole Indians. But after they reached the Pensacola region, Daniel began to change his mind about Florida. The wild land was strangely beautiful, with unusual plants and very few inhabitants. He decided to buy some property and a house.

But Daniel had not forgotten his promise to Rebecca. He wanted to be back in North Carolina in time for Christmas. And he was. Just as his family was sitting down to dinner, Daniel burst through the door. His children were fascinated by his stories of the strange land he had visited. But Rebecca was not at all happy when she heard that her husband had actually bought property and planned to move there. In fact, she absolutely refused to leave her relatives and friends. Fortunately, Daniel lost his enthusiasm, too. He decided he would be just as happy to have something besides alligators to hunt! Florida was forgotten.

Before long, Daniel had developed a new interest. He began to take his ten-year-old son James on hunting trips. He enjoyed teaching his young son the skills needed in the wilderness. He showed him how to tell directions from the sun and stars. He taught him how to shoot and repair a rifle and how to use a skinning knife and a tomahawk. James learned to recognize the calls of animals and birds and to know the difference between their true calls and the clever imitations of the Indians.

On cold winter nights Daniel and James built a fire beside their shelter. Daniel tucked the flaps of his hunting shirt around the boy to keep him warm while he slept.

One night, while Daniel was camping by himself, he woke with a start. Somebody had pulled off his blanket. He looked up to see a group of Indians staring down at him. "Ah, Wide Mouth," one of the Indians said, "have I got you now?" The Indians often called Daniel Wide Mouth because of his broad grin.

Daniel kept his wits. He offered the Indians some of his food. He discussed hunting and the

30

weather with them and even used Indian sign language. His friendly behavior probably saved his life, but it didn't save his belongings. The Indians took his horse, his skins and furs, and all his equipment. Daniel's weeks of patient hunting had come to nothing.

Even though Daniel could make a good living from hunting, he still had money problems. Frequently his catch was stolen by Indians or destroyed by storms and rock slides. When that happened, he had to buy new supplies and firearms—often on credit or with borrowed money. Much of the time he owed more money than he was able to earn, and sometimes the people he owed money to dragged him into court.

During one of these court appearances, Daniel met a successful young lawyer named Richard Henderson. The two men became good friends, and Henderson often defended Daniel in court when the frontiersman had legal problems.

Daniel discovered that Henderson also wanted to explore Kentucky territory. More important, he had the money to back an expedition. But in 1763, the British government had forbidden colonists to cross the Allegheny Mountains to clear trees, plant crops, or build homes. Henderson knew that this order was not realistic. There was no way to keep settlers from moving west. Many veterans of the French and Indian War had already been given land west of the mountains. Still, this order was the law.

Starting in 1764, Henderson paid Daniel Boone to make a few secret scouting trips through eastern Tennessee. He was to look for rich, fertile lands that would be easy to plant. On one trip Daniel and his companions actually reached Kentucky, but they didn't realize it. Daniel killed his first buffalo there. Then a heavy blizzard hit, and the men were forced back to North Carolina.

But Daniel still had "Kentucky fever." He would not be satisfied until he had explored the forbidden territory for himself.

Adventures in Kentucky

One day an unexpected visitor stopped at the Boone cabin. He was John Findley. Daniel hadn't seen him in fourteen years! Findley was now a peddler, traveling around the frontier with a horse and wagon. He sold ribbons, threads, and other household supplies to frontier women.

Findley had been looking for Daniel. He wanted to talk him into going on an expedition to the Kentucky territory. Daniel invited Findley to stay at the Boone cabin for a while. Every night the two men sat by the fireplace swapping yarns and dreaming dreams of a wonderful life in Kentucky. It reminded Daniel of the nights they had spent beside the campfire while serving under General Braddock. Sometimes Daniel's brother Squire and brother-in-law John Stuart joined them.

Findley knew about a special route to Kentucky through the Cumberland Mountains. It was part of Warrior's Path. For generations the Cherokee had followed the secret trail to attack the Shawnee. Lately the Cherokee had used it to raid frontier settlements.

To make his journey, Findley needed the skill of a hunter like Daniel who knew the wilderness well. He also needed money to finance the expedition.

Daniel decided to ask his friend Richard Henderson for help. Henderson was excited about the trip and agreed to supply the money. But he reminded Daniel that the British had promised the land of Kentucky to the Cherokee. The expedition must be kept a complete secret, or they could all be in big trouble with the British government.

One May morning in 1769, the exploring party gathered in front of the Boone cabin. The men were all on horseback, with a blanket, a bearskin, and a packet of food strapped behind each saddle. Extra packhorses were loaded with rifles, traps, bullets, and pots and pans.

Family and friends crowded around to see them off. Rebecca and Hannah Stuart waved as the men rode away. They must have wondered if they would ever see their husbands again.

Daniel, Findley, and Stuart were in the lead. Behind them rode three camp helpers. They were hired to guard the campsite, cook the food, skin the game, and cure and store the skins and furs. Squire Boone remained behind to look after the three farms. He would plant and harvest the summer crops before he set out with fresh supplies and ammunition. No one seemed to question how he would find the others deep in the wilderness of Kentucky!

The first part of the journey was not too difficult. Both Stuart and Daniel knew the country well. They picked out the best and safest trails. After long days of traveling over rough, rugged land, the party approached the Powell River valley. Here they found the last lonely frontier outpost, known as Martin's Station. Beyond this point they would be riding into unknown territory.

Findley was the only one in the group who had any knowledge of the country they were now entering. He led the little band to the famous Warrior's Path where trees grew so thick that the men couldn't see the sky. The group passed through rocky gorges with crashing waterfalls. At any moment unfriendly Indians might silently appear to ambush them.

One day the men found themselves in front of a steep mountain wall of solid white rock. There seemed to be no way over or around it. They began to wonder if Findley really knew what he was talking about. Then suddenly to one side they discovered a break in the wall. They had finally reached the famous Cumberland Gap. They were now at the gateway to Kentucky.

The men traveled north until they reached a fork in the Kentucky River. Here they decided to set up a permanent camp. They called it Station

Camp. They built a simple log shelter near their campfire and prepared to settle in. So far they had been lucky. They hadn't met any Indians— friendly or unfriendly. The tribes were probably hunting game in some other part of the region.

For the next month Daniel explored on his own. One day he reached Big Hill, between the Rockcastle and Kentucky rivers. From the hilltop he looked down at rich, rolling land. All the hard work and all his dreaming had finally brought him to his goal.

When Daniel returned, the men knew it was time to do some serious hunting. Daniel went off with John Stuart, and Findley hunted with one of the camp helpers. Each pair set up small temporary camps far from Station Camp. As soon as they had a good supply of game, they would take it back to the main camp. There the camp helpers would dry the meat and scrape and cure the skins. Then they would pile the skins and furs onto log platforms out of the reach of wolves and bears.

Since they hadn't seen any Indians, the hunters became careless. They forgot that Station Camp was dangerously close to Warrior's Path. One morning a group of Shawnee men on horseback took Daniel and Stuart by surprise. The two hunters looked up to discover the Indians aiming their rifles, ready to fire. Daniel tried his usual trick of starting a friendly conversation. But the Shawnee leader, Captain Will, wasn't fooled. He told Dan-

36

iel to lead him to the hunters' main camp. He wanted all the furs and animal skins that the white hunters had taken from his Shawnee brothers.

Daniel didn't panic. He quickly thought of a scheme to fool the Indians. He would take them to another temporary camp. The hunter at that camp would hear the Indians approaching. He could rush off to Station Camp to warn the others. The men would have a chance to pack up the skins and escape with the horses.

The trick didn't work. Instead of trying to save the skins, the camp workers rushed off into the woods to hide. There was nothing for Findley to do but follow them. When the Shawnee men rode into Station Camp with their two prisoners, they seized everything, including the horses. Six long months of work had been lost.

Captain Will was so pleased with what he had taken that he decided to let Daniel and Stuart go. He even gave each of them a small rifle and enough ammunition to get home safely. But before releasing them, he gave the hunters a stern lecture. "Don't come here anymore," he warned. "This is the *Indians'* hunting ground, and all the animals, skins, and furs are ours."

Daniel didn't agree. He felt they had been robbed. He believed that wild game belonged to whoever shot it. Instead of heading back home, he and Stuart decided to follow the Shawnee's trail. Maybe they could at least get their horses back!

Two nights later the hunters discovered the Indians fast asleep at their overnight campsite. Quietly they freed five of their horses and galloped off through the forest. At dawn they finally stopped to give the horses some water and a chance to rest. Daniel had just stretched out on a grassy riverbank when a group of Shawnee suddenly rode over the hills. The two hunters were prisoners again!

Captain Will scolded the men for trying to steal the horses. But he was so happy to have tricked Daniel that he didn't harm the hunters. As punishment for their foolishness, he tied bells around their necks and made them prance around like horses. The bells rang merrily while the Indians stood around laughing at the sight.

This time Captain Will was taking no chances. He told the two hunters he would escort them all the way to the Ohio River. Then they couldn't bother him any longer. But while the Indians were setting up camp for the night, Daniel noticed that some guns had been left unguarded. He nudged Stuart and nodded in the direction of the rifles. When Daniel gave the signal, the two men leaped to their feet. Each of them grabbed a gun and dashed into a nearby canebrake.

By the time the Indians gave chase, the two hunters had completely disappeared in the tall, thick reeds. The Shawnee searched for them but finally gave up. The next afternoon they rode away to join the rest of their tribe. Daniel and

S.J.PETRUCCIO

Stuart started back to Station Camp. They hoped they would find the other men there.

At twilight Daniel and Stuart saw a fire in the distance. Six people were sitting around it eating, but Daniel could not see them clearly through the trees. He shouted out, "Strangers, who are you?"

"White men and friends," answered a familiar voice. Daniel was in luck. Not only had he found Findley and the three camp workers, but his brother Squire was there as well, with a friend.

No sight could have been more welcome. Squire and his companion, Alexander Neely, were loaded down with supplies, guns, and ammunition. They had also brought extra horses. But despite these new supplies, Findley had had enough. He was tired and sick. He realized that he was just too old for such an expedition. The three camp workers wanted to return home, too. So the four men departed the next day, leaving the Boone brothers with Stuart and Neely. The four hunters established a new camp at a safe distance from Warrior's Path. When they went out to set their traps, they worked in pairs. Squire went with Neely; Daniel worked with Stuart.

In January, Daniel and Stuart decided to split up for a week. On the day they were to meet, Stuart failed to appear. For days Daniel wandered through the forest calling to his friend. But there was no answer. At last he gave up and returned to camp to tell the others. Neely immediately decided to go back to North Carolina. Kentucky was not for him!

Five years later, Daniel found Stuart's powder horn in the area where they had been hunting. He looked around and there, sitting inside a hollow tree, was a human skeleton! The skeleton had a broken left arm. Daniel had finally solved the mystery of Stuart's death. He had been shot by Indians. He had probably run away from them, but by the time he reached this clearing, he must have been too weak to go any farther.

The two Boone brothers were now on their own. They continued to hunt, but they were very careful. They cooked at night so the Indians wouldn't see the smoke. They even hid the entrance to their camp. By spring they began to run out of ammunition. Squire volunteered to return east for a new supply. He loaded their skins onto a packhorse. The skins would help pay Daniel's debts and buy new supplies.

Daniel was all alone in the wilderness. He didn't even have a horse or a dog. But for the next three months he continued to explore. He felt he owed it to Henderson to see as much territory as possible. At night he slept in canebrakes so the Indians couldn't find him. Sometimes he camped in caves. In fact, years later, someone found carved on a cave wall the message D.B.—1770.

Squire made a safe journey to Salisbury, on the Yadkin River in central North Carolina. He returned in July with a load of supplies. He also brought good news. Daniel had a third son, Daniel Morgan, born just before Christmas. With the new supply of ammunition, the brothers were able to hunt again. By fall there were more skins for Squire to take to Salisbury. Daniel felt the trip was turning into a success. Soon they would be able to return to their families.

In March 1771, they started the final trip east. Their horses were loaded with skins. All went well until they reached the Cumberland Gap, where they stopped to eat. Suddenly a group of Indians appeared. They seemed friendly, so Daniel invited them to share the fresh meat he was roasting. The Indians ate, but when they were finished, they ordered the hunters to turn over all their skins, guns, and supplies. Outnumbered, the brothers had to give the Indians everything. Once again they had lost six months' hard work. Even with the two loads of furs that Squire had already sold, Daniel still owed money to just about everybody in town.

But Daniel had something that *nobody* could take from him. He knew all about a land few white settlers had ever seen.

Daniel went home, happy to see his family again, but he could hardly wait to get back to Kentucky. He had fallen in love with the land.

A Tragedy in the Wilderness

Daniel had been back in North Carolina for two years. For months he had dreamed of returning to Kentucky with his family, but Henderson told him it wasn't the right time to settle the territory. Instead he sent Daniel on more missions—usually to talk to friendly Indian chiefs about selling land.

On his last mission into the wilderness, Daniel stopped at the small western Virginia settlement of Castle's Woods in the Clinch River valley. Here he met the settlement's founder, Captain William Russell. For fighting in the French and Indian War, Russell had received a big piece of land in Kentucky, though he had never been there.

Daniel told him all about the wonders of the land—his favorite subject. His descriptions were so glowing that Russell decided to start a new settlement there himself.

Daniel rushed home to tell Rebecca to begin packing. He sold his farm and all his land, as well as any possessions they couldn't take with them. Daniel's enthusiasm quickly spread. Five families, including his brother Squire's, agreed to go along. Some of Rebecca's relatives arranged to join them along the way. In Castle's Woods, Captain Russell was forming another group.

There were many reasons why settlers were so eager to move to the wilderness beyond the mountains. Many had huge debts they wanted to escape. Quitrent—money colonial landowners had to pay the British government—kept most colonists poor. Others were fed up with British taxes and dishonest royal governors. And some— like Daniel—just wanted to go where no settlers had ever been before.

This time the settlers couldn't take covered wagons. The trails were too narrow and rough. Supplies had to be bundled onto the backs of packhorses. Children too small to walk were tucked between the soft bundles.

Pans clanged and jangled as the horses moved forward. Butter churns rattled in small carts pulled by strong bulls. One packhorse carried on its back all that a single family would have to wear, eat, cook, and farm with for a whole year. The men, and most of the women, walked alongside the horses. The older children were responsible for keeping the stubborn cows moving through the wilderness.

There were many sad faces when the caravan

set out from the Yadkin Valley on September 26, 1773. Many knew they might never see their friends and relatives again.

At two arranged meeting places, the other parties joined the Boones. The long caravan was split into three groups. Daniel was up front with the Yadkin families. Behind them, James Boone and Captain Russell's oldest son, Henry, tended a herd of cattle. Both boys were about sixteen. Two younger boys were with them, as well as two young black slaves and two hired helpers. Captain Russell and his group were in the rear.

About a day's walk from the Cumberland Gap, Daniel decided the party should stop for the night. The three groups were some distance apart. The boys spread their blankets near a stream where the cattle could drink. After building a campfire, they ate supper, then curled up in their blankets. During the night they heard wolves howling. The boys were afraid that Indians were making the sounds. They huddled closer together in the darkness.

Just before sunrise a band of painted Shawnee crept out of the woods. They were armed with guns, bows and arrows, knives, and tomahawks. The boys never had a chance. Nearly everyone was killed. One slave, named Adam, survived by hiding in some driftwood along the creek.

The deadly massacre turned everyone except Daniel against Kentucky. The grieving party had no wish to continue the journey. After burying the boys in a wilderness grave, they started back to Virginia.

James's death was a dreadful blow to Daniel. The two had always been very close. But he and Rebecca had sold their home and most of their belongings. Where could they go? When Daniel was offered the use of a cabin in Castle's Woods, he was glad to accept.

News of the murders quickly spread through the border settlements. People were outraged. Some white settlers went so far as to provoke incidents with Indians, then kill them as a kind of revenge. Tempers were running high. Governor Dunmore of Virginia secretly stirred up the Indians. He made them hate the white settlers even more. Then, when the angry Indians attacked, the governor had an excuse to send troops to wipe out the warring tribes. These battles were called Lord Dunmore's War.

In Castle's Woods, Daniel was given a new job. A party of surveyors had gone down the Ohio River to explore the territory. They had no way of knowing about the new wave of Indian uprisings. Unless someone warned them and guided them to safety, they might never come back alive. Daniel and another man from Castle's Woods, Michael Stoner, went to look for them. Their search took them through four hundred miles of trackless wilderness, but they found the surveyors and brought them unharmed through hostile Indian territory. Daniel and Stoner had covered eight hundred miles in just sixty days.

When Daniel and Stoner returned, they found that most of the men in the Clinch River valley were gone. They had left to fight in Lord Dunmore's War. Daniel and Stoner wanted to go too, but Captain Russell asked them to stay behind to protect the houses and farms.

Three small forts had already been built along the Clinch River. One of these forts was Moore's Fort. This was where Daniel's family lived during the war. Daniel was put in charge of all three and given the title of captain. His appointment helped to calm the settlers' fears. They knew that Daniel would do everything possible to protect them since his own family lived there.

Daniel took his duties seriously, but some of the other men didn't. One day while he was visiting another fort, the guards at Moore's Fort went outside to enjoy the autumn sun. Some played ball. Others stretched out on the grass or swam in a nearby pond. Their rifles were lying here and there in the grass. Such carelessness angered Rebecca Boone. It was dangerous, and they were disobeying Daniel's orders.

She and several other women decided to teach the men a lesson. They loaded some guns with a small amount of powder so they would sound like Indian guns. Then they sneaked out to the far

side of the fort, where they fired rapidly. The men couldn't see them. They thought Indians had attacked. They tried to run back to the fort, but the doors were locked. The women had raced back inside and slammed them shut.

In a panic the men ran in every direction. Some even dived into the pond with their clothes on. When the guards discovered Rebecca's trick, they were furious. But they had learned a valuable lesson. After that, they took their guard duty more seriously.

Finally Lord Dunmore defeated the Shawnee. Richard Henderson decided that the time was right to settle the Kentucky territory. He wanted to buy twenty million acres of land directly from the Cherokee. With this land he planned to create a new, fourteenth colony. It would be called Transylvania. Many people in the colonies thought he had lost his mind—the scheme was so bold, so daring, and so illegal.

Henderson, who had become a judge by this time, didn't care. He was sick of the British and their rules. Months earlier, some colonists had dumped three shiploads of British tea into the Boston Harbor. Henderson admired these men. They had been protesting unfair taxes. He knew that the frontier settlers hated British taxes and rules too.

Henderson and some other men formed the Transylvania Company. This company sent Daniel on a new mission to Kentucky. For five months he met with all the friendly Cherokee chiefs again, explaining Henderson's offer. He told them that Henderson and his partners wanted to *buy* their land. They weren't trying to steal it, as others had. To further impress the Indians, Henderson and his partners sent six wagons full of guns, colored shirts, blankets, earrings, and tools to the ancient Cherokee treaty grounds at Sycamore Shoals. The company was willing to pay the Indians fifty thousand dollars in goods. In exchange, the Transylvania Company would own a large part of what is now Kentucky and Tennessee. Quite a bargain—for Henderson and his friends!

More than a thousand Cherokee gathered for the official signing of the treaty on March 17, 1775.

Not all of the Indians approved. Dragging Canoe, the son of Chief Atacullaculla, objected. He said, "The whites have passed the mountains and settled upon Cherokee lands, and now wish a treaty. When they are unable to point out any further retreat for the miserable Cherokee, they will proclaim the extinction of the whole race." Dragging Canoe finally agreed to the treaty, but he warned that there might still be trouble. This trouble, he predicted, would not come from the Cherokee but from the angry Shawnee to the north.

Kidnapped!

Before the treaty with the Cherokee had been signed, Daniel left to start work on a road to Kentucky. Thirty men had been hired to help with the job. They were waiting for him at the Holston River. Daniel's brother Squire and a neighbor from North Carolina—Colonel Richard Callaway—were part of the road-cutting crew.

The new Wilderness Road would be a 250-mile-long dirt trail, just wide enough for packhorses and small ox carts. It would run from the Holston River, in what is now northeastern Tennessee, to the banks of the Kentucky River. All day long the road cutters chopped away at thick canes, brush, and trees, following Indian trails, buffalo paths, and river valleys. The work was hard, but the job went well. The men respected Daniel as a leader and worked well for him. When the crew finally reached the rolling bluegrass country of Kentucky, they were amazed. They had never before seen such rich soil or so much wild game.

Then trouble struck. They were camped for the night just fifteen miles from their final destination. Early in the morning the sound of gunfire boomed through the camp. A band of Shawnee had attacked. The men dashed for the safety of the woods, many without stopping to pick up their guns. Most of them managed to escape, but two were wounded. One died later that day. The Indians dashed away as quickly as they had appeared, taking some horses and supplies with them.

Some of the road cutters were so frightened that they packed their belongings and headed back east. But Daniel convinced most of the men to continue with him. The road was almost finished. By April 1, 1775, the crew reached the place Daniel had chosen for a settlement. It was on the banks of the Kentucky River. The road cutters had reached their goal in just over three weeks.

The men began chopping down trees and building a few rough cabins. But soon their interest turned to getting good land for themselves. Everywhere men were surveying land, pacing off plots, or chasing after the buffalo that grazed in the area. They were so busy that they forgot to keep a lookout for hostile Indians. One man who wandered off by himself was killed by a band of roving Shawnee.

On April 20, Henderson arrived with a caravan

of almost fifty men on horseback There were also packhorses loaded with ammunition, seed corn, and other supplies, and a herd of cattle. Daniel and his men were happy to see the others and greeted the newcomers by firing twenty-five rifles. Nobody at the celebration knew what was happening back east. Just the day before colonists had fired on British soldiers in the towns of Lexington and Concord, Massachusetts. Back east, the colonies were getting closer and closer to war with their mother country.

Henderson didn't like the location of the new settlement. He thought the site would be hard to defend. He also wasn't very pleased to find that the men had named the settlement Boonesborough. He wanted it to be called Hendersonville! But he saw how much the men respected Daniel, so he kept quiet. He only suggested that they build a fort a little farther up the river.

In late April work began on the new fort. It was going to be built in the shape of a rectangle. The two longer walls would measure about 250 feet and run parallel to the river. The shorter walls would measure about seventy-five feet. To make the walls, the men stuck heavy logs upright in the earth. The logs were pointed at the top. At each of the four corners of the fort, they were going to build guard towers. From these towers riflemen and lookouts could watch the countryside and guard the fort.

Work progressed slowly. Henderson had many problems to settle. He was upset that the road crew had taken the best land for themselves. He wanted to hold a lottery to divide up the property more fairly. He also told the settlers that they had to start planting crops at once or there would be no food for winter. Every week more and more settlers were traveling the Wilderness Road to Kentucky. And one day Henderson was astonished to learn that a man named James Harrod had already started a settlement nearby called Harrodsburg. Harrod claimed to have been granted the land by the colony of Pennsylvania. But Harrodsburg was part of Transylvania, which Henderson had bought from the Cherokee!

Instead of arguing over who owned the land, Henderson decided to include everybody in his colony of Transylvania. He held a big meeting under a giant elm tree and told everyone how he intended to run the colony. His ideas were not very popular. For one thing, he and his partners wanted each man to pay a quitrent for his property. Settlers who had left the east just to avoid paying a quitrent were angry about this. Henderson also announced that he and his partners would choose the leaders of the new colony. There would be no democratic vote.

Daniel was unhappy because settlers were killing more game than they needed. The buffalo herds were disappearing from the area. Hunters

54

had to go farther and farther to find game—sometimes thirty miles or more. He proposed a bill for protecting game, and the bill became a law. But by June, Daniel was tired of the arguing. He decided to return to Virginia for his family.

While Daniel was gone, Henderson had trouble getting the men to do anything. Daniel was the only leader they trusted. Finally Henderson gave up. He went back east to prove to the Continental Congress that his company owned the land. The Continental Congress was a meeting in Philadelphia of representatives from the thirteen colonies. They had gathered to discuss their problems with England.

Daniel returned in September, bringing Rebecca and six of his children with him. He also brought twenty young men who wanted to settle at Boonesborough. They were a welcome sight with their cattle, hogs, dogs, and chickens. They also had packhorses loaded with much-needed supplies and ammunition.

Rebecca and thirteen-year-old Jemima Boone were the first women to join the Boonesborough settlement. Although Rebecca was used to frontier life, she wasn't quite ready for what she saw. There were only a few cabins, and most of them had never been finished. Several were completely open on one side. Others were missing doors and windows. In all her years of living with Daniel, she had never been so far from civilization. No stores, no churches, no real neighboring villages.

Rebecca had never been a person to complain, and she didn't start now. She settled her family in their crude little cabin built in a hollow outside the fort. All the cabins were dark and drafty, with hard-packed dirt floors. There was no glass in the windows—sometimes there was no window. Often the only light in Rebecca's cabin came from the fireplace.

Rebecca must have been delighted the day that Colonel Callaway arrived with his wife and two daughters, Betsey and Fanny. Betsey was sixteen and Fanny was fourteen. Soon other families made the trip, including some of Rebecca's relatives.

The Boones decided to move to a cabin inside the fort. Things had become more civilized there. A few people had soap kettles and clotheslines—even a spinning wheel or two.

The fort had one big drawback. It contained no well or other source of fresh water. If Indians attacked, the settlers would have to depend on catching rainwater in buckets.

One warm Sunday afternoon in July, Daniel was taking a nap in his cabin. His daughter Jemima and the two Callaway girls decided to go for a canoe ride down the river. Jemima had cut her foot on a sharp broken cane stalk, so Betsey and Fanny paddled while she dangled her sore foot in the cold water. Gradually the canoe drifted toward the opposite shore. The girls talked about getting out to pick wildflowers in the woods. Jemima thought it would be too dangerous. Indians often prowled around among the thick trees and bushes.

Suddenly a swift river current drove the canoe into the bank. Before they could pry it loose, a group of Indians crashed through the dense cane. Snatching at the canoe, they pulled it onto the shore. Then they grabbed the three girls. Fanny Callaway shrieked "Indians!" and tried to hit them with her paddle. But the Indians clapped their hands over the girls' mouths and ordered them to be quiet. Waving their knives and tomahawks, they dragged the girls up the bank into the woods.

Jemima threw herself on the ground, complaining that she couldn't walk another step. She showed them the cane wound on her foot. The Indians gave her a pair of moccasins and ordered her to move along.

But the three frontier girls had some tricks of their own. As they trudged through the thick trees, they left a trail behind them. They broke twigs from the bushes and tore pieces of cloth from their skirts to drop along the trail. Betsey dug her heels into the soft dirt as often as she dared. At one point she even dropped a handkerchief with CALLAWAY stitched on it. Every so often Jemima would fall to the ground, moaning about the pain in her foot.

When night fell, the Indians stopped to rest. They didn't dare light a fire in case a rescue party was hunting for them. The girls were tied with their backs against the trees. None of them got much sleep that night. Jemima was wondering if her father would be able to find them. She had watched the Indians making false trails to fool anyone who tried to follow them.

There were just five Indians—two Shawnee and three Cherokee. Hanging Maw, a Cherokee chief, was the leader. Jemima recognized the chief. She had seen him with her father back in North Carolina. When she told him who she was, he was delighted. "You Wide Mouth's daughter?" he exclaimed. She nodded, then told him that the other two girls were her sisters. She thought Hanging Maw might treat them better if he thought they were Daniel Boone's daughters. Hanging Maw was doubly pleased when he heard the news. White female prisoners were always a special prize, but three daughters of Wide Mouth would be even better.

The next day Jemima complained so much about her foot that the Indians put her on a pony. Hanging Maw wanted get back to the camp as soon as possible. No rescue party—not even one led by Daniel Boone—could free the girls there. But the pony didn't help. When the Indians weren't looking, the girls would poke it with a stick. Then the pony would rear up, throwing Jemima to the ground. Finally it ran away.

By the second night Jemima was losing hope. Even with her tricks the Indians had covered a lot of ground. How could her father find her now?

Jemima should have known better. Daniel had wasted no time as soon as he learned that the three girls were missing. The instant he saw the empty canoe, he knew what had happened. As quickly as possible he organized a rescue party. Sam Henderson, a younger brother of Richard, was first to volunteer. He was engaged to marry Betsey Callaway. But the rescue party didn't get very far on Sunday. Darkness came too quickly. All day Monday, however, they followed the trail the girls had left. Daniel wasn't fooled by the Indians' false trails.

At noon on Tuesday, Daniel and his men smelled smoke. They discovered muddy tracks leading from a little creek. Sneaking through the thick brush, they found the Indians' camp. The Indians were getting ready to roast a piece of buffalo meat. The three girls sat under a tree. Jemima and Fanny had their heads in Betsey's lap.

Daniel sent half his men around to the rear of the camp. He did this so the Indians couldn't escape with the girls. At a signal—Boone's rifle shot—the men rushed at the Indians, firing their guns.

When Jemima heard the shots, she jumped up. "That's Daddy!" she cried out.

Taken by surprise, the Indians made one unsuccessful attempt to grab the girls, then rushed off into the canebrakes without them. Jemima and her friends were safe.

News of the dramatic rescue spread across the frontier. In fact, it caused a lot more excitement than the news from the east. The Continental Congress had issued a declaration of independence just two weeks earlier. The colonies had separated from Great Britain.

A Prisoner of the Indians

The Revolutionary War—the war between England and the colonies—brought new troubles for Kentucky settlers. The British became allies of the Indians. They gave them guns, artillery, and other gifts as payment for attacking settlers in Kentucky and the Ohio Valley. No one was safe against the fierce surprise raids of the Shawnee. They stole horses, killed cattle, and set fire to crops growing in the fields. They even threw flaming firebrands into the cabins and killed farmers and hunters who were alone and unprotected in the woods. Food became a real problem. There was little to eat except turnips and cornmeal mush. Now and then men went out hunting at night, hoping the Indians wouldn't find them.

People who lived in outlying cabins had to move back to the forts. Some people moved all the way back east. Seven settlements were completely abandoned. Only the three strongest forts remained: Boonesborough, Harrodsburg, and Logan's Station. Boone, Harrod, and Logan were made captains of their forts. Of the five hundred settlers who had come to Kentucky, only about two hundred remained. And just twelve of these were women. The fearless Rebecca and Jemima Boone were among them.

Under the country's new independent government, Kentucky was now a county of Virginia. But instead of sending help, the Virginia officials ordered most Kentucky men to serve in the Continental army. Daniel instructed the remaining men to strengthen Boonesborough's fort. There were still many gaps in the walls, and two of the towers had never been finished.

In April 1777, Chief Blackfish attacked the fort with fifty of his Shawnee warriors. Some of the men were outside the fort when the war party struck. A bullet hit Daniel in the ankle. He had to be carried back inside by a friend. Fortunately, no one was killed. But the settlers were more nervous than ever.

Finally Major William Bailey Smith arrived with a group of armed volunteers. Most of the newcomers were old friends and neighbors of the Boones from the Yadkin Valley. They were carrying the new red, white, and blue American flag with thirteen stars. The Boonesborough settlers had never seen it before. Soon the flag was flying over the fort.

For a few months the settlers relaxed. With the additional protection, they were able to plant and harvest crops. Some men even went into the woods to hunt. But in the fall the volunteers had to leave. Only Major Smith remained. The people of Boonesborough were on their own again. And now they had a new problem. They had run out of salt. Without salt they couldn't cure skins and preserve meat for the winter. If they didn't have meat, they would starve.

Daniel knew where there were some underground saltwater springs. In a few places the salty water bubbled up through the limestone. Buffalo and other animals often came there to lick the salt-covered rocks. These places were called licks. The nearest one—Lower Blue Licks—was about forty miles away. In early January, Daniel went there with about thirty men to collect salt.

Collecting salt was a difficult job. The men had to chop wood and keep fires blazing. They boiled water in huge kettles until nothing but the precious white salt crystals remained. It took more than eight hundred gallons of saltwater to make one bushel—a basket—of salt.

Daniel wasn't too worried about Indian attacks. He knew that the Shawnee spent the cold months in their winter camps far from Boonesborough. Still, he assigned three scouts to keep watch in the surrounding forest while the men boiled the water in their salt kettles. After a few weeks, they had about three hundred bushels of salt to send back to the fort.

Early in February, Daniel decided to take a break from salt-making. Since there had been no signs of Indians, he wanted to do some hunting and check his beaver traps. About ten miles from camp, he shot a buffalo. He strapped the carcass to his packhorse and started back to camp. Just then a heavy snow began to fall. He had trouble seeing anything around him, but he sensed that he was being followed. He looked behind him and saw four well-armed Indians closing in. There was no way he could escape. So he stood his rifle against a tree and surrendered.

His Shawnee captors led him over the snow to their camp. It was only about an hour away. At the camp Daniel was surprised to find a heavily armed war party of more than one hundred Shawnee and Delaware warriors. He recognized some of them, including Captain Will, who had tied horse bells on him and made him dance. Chief Blackfish was the leader of the war party.

A few months earlier, an important Shawnee chief named Cornstalk had been murdered by some soldiers at Fort Randolph, located a few miles from Point Pleasant, a settlement on the Ohio River in what is now West Virginia. Three other chiefs had been killed at the same time. The killings had angered the Shawnee because their leaders had gone unarmed to the fort for a peace meeting. Now Daniel learned that the Shawnee were seeking revenge. They planned to destroy Fort Boonesborough. Then they were going to attack Harrodsburg and Logan's Station.

Daniel had to think fast. Most of the best riflemen were at the salt lick. There weren't enough men left at Boonesborough to defend the fort. But he didn't want Chief Blackfish to know that. Instead he advised the chief not to try to take the fort. He told him he would find too large a force there—at least sixty men. The chief would be wiser to send a party to capture the men at the salt lick. The Indians could ransom the prisoners to the British. Then in the spring, when the weather was better, Daniel promised that he would lead Blackfish's warriors to Boonesborough.

Daniel said he would lead the Indians to the salt licks, but he asked for one thing in return. He made Blackfish promise that the men would not have to "run the gauntlet" at the Indian camp. Running the gauntlet was an Indian tradition when prisoners arrived at their village. All the villagers stood in two lines, armed with clubs, sticks, rocks, or poles. The prisoners had to run between the two lines while the Indians struck them with their weapons. If a prisoner didn't run fast enough, he could be seriously hurt or killed. Chief Blackfish gave his word that Daniel's friends would not have to run the gauntlet if they surrendered without a fight.

The next morning Daniel led a large party of warriors to the salt licks. Snow was still falling, so the Shawnee surrounded the camp without being seen or heard. Then Blackfish sent Daniel to talk to his men. Two Indians walked behind him with their rifles pointed at his back. When the work party saw the armed Indians, they started to grab their weapons. Daniel warned them that they were surrounded. There was nothing to do but surrender. He explained that the Indians had promised to treat them well.

The stunned salt workers realized that they had no choice. They stacked their weapons in a pile. The Indians collected the settlers' rifles, horses, and kettles. Then, shouting gleefully, they scattered three hundred bushels of precious salt all over the snow.

At last the party trudged off into the white forest. The Kentuckians walked single file, carrying their supplies. They were puzzled when they noticed that Daniel didn't have to carry anything. He was treated differently. They began to wonder: had he really been forced to surrender the other salt workers, or did he do it just to save his own life?

At dusk the party stopped to camp for the night. The Indians began to tramp down a long clearing in the snow. Daniel immediately understood what they were doing. He reminded the chief that he had promised not to make the men run the gauntlet. Blackfish smiled. He had promised that the *men* would not be forced to run the gauntlet, but he hadn't said anything about Daniel! Daniel couldn't argue. He knew he had been outwitted.

Daniel watched the warriors line up. Then, without any warning, he lowered his head and rushed between the lines. Fists, clubs, switches, and tomahawk butts struck at him while he danced from side to side, trying to avoid the full force of the blows. He charged right into the stomach of one surprised man, knocking him to the snow. The Shawnee laughed and cheered, and Blackfish watched Daniel with admiration. He had already decided that the brave frontiersman would make a worthy adopted son for him.

At their main camp the Shawnee kept sixteen of the prisoners as adopted members of the tribe. The rest were taken to Fort Detroit to be ransomed to the British. During the following weeks, Daniel seemed to fit right in to the tribe's daily routine. He hunted and practiced target shooting with the Shawnee men. He repaired their rifles and laughed and joked with them. As far as anyone could see, he was perfectly happy with his new life. Some of the other Boonesborough men watched him with disgust, but the Indians respected him. They observed that he never killed just for sport, but only to get food or to defend himself. Like the Indians, he had a great respect for the land and the animals that lived on it. He knew the Indians could be cruel and savage, but he also knew that the colonists had done many things to provoke such behavior.

In the spring, Chief Blackfish felt it was time to adopt Daniel in a special ceremony. But first Daniel had to be prepared. Except for a four-inch scalp lock, all the hair was plucked from Daniel's head. Then he was taken to the river and undressed. Some old Indian women scrubbed him hard from head to foot until his skin was raw. This was to "take all his white blood out." Afterward, his head and face were painted with symbols of the tribe. He was given a new Indian name—*Sheltowee,* which meant "Big Turtle." After the ceremony, the Indian warriors smoked a pipe with their new brother, and everyone feasted on venison, corn, and maple sugar.

Daniel realized that the Indians still didn't trust him completely. They watched him whenever he left camp or took his horse out to pasture. He was never allowed to hunt by himself and he was never permitted to keep unused bullets. He was very careful not to do anything that would make them suspicious. He never gave the slightest hint that he might try to escape. But that's all he was thinking about. He managed to sneak out some of the gunpowder they gave him, and he sometimes cut his bullets in two so he could keep half.

In June a Shawnee war party rode into the

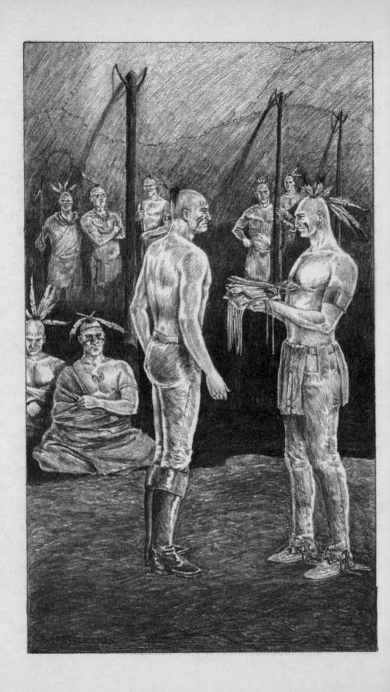

camp. They had just been badly beaten in a series of battles in western Virginia. The news angered Chief Blackfish and his men. The chief announced that he was going to launch an attack on Boonesborough right away.

Daniel knew that the time had come for him to make his escape. His friends and family at the fort must be warned at once. He waited until the Shawnee men were all out hunting. Then he gathered up his secret supply of bullets and food, grabbed a rifle and a horse, and galloped out of the camp as fast as he could. All day he guided the horse along streambeds so he would leave no trail. When darkness came, he kept going.

In the morning the horse was too tired to travel any farther. Daniel continued on foot. He didn't stop until he reached the Ohio River. He made a crude raft to cross the water, landing many miles downstream. Finally he felt safe enough to rest. On June 20—four days after his escape—he reached the Kentucky River. He had made a remarkable journey: 160 miles in just four days, mostly on foot.

When he arrived at the fort, no one recognized him. He was still dressed like an Indian. The only hair on his head was the scalp lock that the Indians had left. The settlers were astonished when Daniel told them all that had happened to him. Rebecca, they said, had gone back to North Carolina with the children. She was certain that Daniel was dead. Only Jemima remained at the fort. And now she was the wife of Flanders Callaway.

Daniel went to the old cabin, but the only one there to greet him was the family cat. She at least seemed happy to see him again.

The Siege of Boonesborough

Daniel warned his old friends that the Indians might attack the fort any day. He agreed to stay there to help instead of going back to North Carolina for his family. There was a lot of work to be done. The big double gates wouldn't shut. Two of the guard towers still hadn't been completed, and there were big holes in the walls.

On July 17, 1778, another captured salt worker arrived, exhausted, at the gate. His name was William Hancock. He had also managed to escape from Blackfish's camp. He brought word that the Shawnee now planned to attack during late July. They had gathered a force of more than four hundred fighting men, and the British had supplied them with four cannons. Hancock's stories about Daniel's treatment while he was a prisoner of the Shawnee aroused some suspicion. Colonel Callaway was jealous of Daniel's popularity, so he eagerly spread rumors about Daniel that weren't true. Fortunately, most of the settlers trusted Daniel more than Callaway.

By late August the Shawnee had still not attacked. Daniel decided to spy on the Indians. He and his scouting party raided a few small Indian camps, but none had many warriors in them. Daniel figured that they must already be gathering somewhere. Daniel decided to return to the fort right away. On the way he spied a huge war party of Indians in the woods. They were covering themselves with bright war paint. And they had a great supply of scalping knives. The scouting party raced back to the fort to warn the others.

The fort went on the alert. Some people collected food from the surrounding fields. Others chopped wood and filled buckets with fresh spring water. The men cleaned their rifles and measured out gunpowder. They were assigned places inside the fort. Women and boys would stand beside them, reloading rifles. The fort had a pitifully small fighting force—only thirty men and twenty boys, plus a few women, girls, and slaves. How could they possibly hold out against four hundred well-armed attackers?

Early on the morning of September 7, the first Indians appeared over the ridge. They crossed the river boldly and rode right up to the fort. Obviously they didn't plan to take the fort by surprise. While lookouts watched anxiously from the guard towers, Indians surrounded the fort. There were Shawnee, Mingo, Wyandot, and Cherokee Indians, along with some French-Canadians and British redcoats carrying French and British flags.

Inside the fort some of the women and old people walked around carrying sticks with fur hats on top of them. Others held rifles up high. Daniel had suggested these tricks. He wanted the Indian scouts watching from the hills to think that there was a big force of fighting men inside. Smoke rose from all the chimneys, giving the impression that life continued as usual.

While the lookouts watched closely, the Indians sent a messenger to the fort gate. He was carrying a white truce flag. When Daniel asked what he wanted, the messenger said that Blackfish had brought letters from Lieutenant Governor Hamilton at Fort Detroit.

Despite the objections of many settlers, Daniel agreed to go outside to talk to Blackfish. The men inside the fort held their rifles at the ready in case the Indians tried any tricks. But the meeting was friendly. Blackfish told Daniel that he had come to take the fort. He handed Daniel the letter from Governor Hamilton. In the letter the governor urged Daniel to surrender. If the settlers surrendered peacefully, they would not be harmed. They would be taken to the main Indian camp and treated well. But if the settlers didn't surrender, the men and children would be killed and the women taken prisoner.

Daniel pretended that he didn't have the authority to answer. He said there was a much higher ranking officer inside the fort, and that officer didn't want to surrender. He would have to go back and talk to him. Daniel was trying to delay the fighting as long as possible. He hoped that any day more fighting men would arrive from North Carolina or Virginia. In the meantime, he offered food and hospitality to the Indians. He wanted them to think that the fort was well supplied.

Later in the day, Daniel reappeared, this time with Major Smith, who was wearing his full-dress uniform. In was an impressive sight to the Indians. Blackfish introduced some of the other important Indian leaders, as well as a lieutenant from the British army.

For two more days Boone and Smith managed to keep the peace talks going. At one point the Indians asked to see Jemima Boone. They had heard the story of her kidnapping and rescue, and they wanted to get a look at her. Some of the settlers feared she would be taken hostage, but Daniel agreed. The gates were opened and Jemima stood there with her husband. The Indians were delighted.

On September 11, 1778, Daniel couldn't stall the Indians any longer. The battle for Boonesborough began. Guns fired, bullets whistled. Behind the locked gates of the fort, dogs howled and cattle stampeded. Frightened children wailed while the women huddled together, waiting for the Indians to come crashing through the fort walls. Daniel seemed to be everywhere, encouraging riflemen, comforting the wounded, and checking on supplies.

By the time the Indians charged the fort, the settlers were ready for them. The riflemen picked their targets with care. The women handed them reloaded guns. After a fierce exchange of gunfire, the Indians finally retreated. The sudden quiet was spooky. Later that night someone spotted flames outside the west wall. The Indians were trying to burn down the fort! Daniel ordered a trench dug under the fort wall. Then two men crawled out and poured water on the flames. Soon the fire died out.

The next morning the Indians rode off, making a good deal of clatter and commotion. But Daniel wasn't fooled. He knew they would be back. Sure enough, back they came. Once again gunfire raged.

A little later the lookouts in the towers noticed that the river had turned brown and muddy. The Indians must be trying something else. The lookouts discovered that the Indians were digging a tunnel from the riverbank to the fort. It was clear that they planned to burrow under one of the walls to make it collapse. Then the warriors would be able to invade the fort in huge numbers.

Daniel quickly came up with a plan. He ordered his men to dig their own tunnel. The passage would run under the wall and cross the Indians' tunnel. This would give the Kentuckians a chance to shoot the invaders as they crawled through. With luck it might even cause their tunnel to collapse.

Digging a tunnel was back-breaking work—especially on a scorching-hot day. The settlers were running out of water and food. But day after day the shooting and the digging continued.

During the night of the sixth day, the Indians made another full-scale attack against the fort. This time they shot burning arrows onto cabin roofs. Then they aimed their rifles at the rooftops, ready to shoot anyone who tried to put out the fires. But the settlers were courageous. They dashed onto the roofs and pulled out burning shingles. But for every fire they managed to put out, two more started somewhere else. With horror, the settlers watched the flames spread to the walls of the fort. Those walls were their only protection. Worse yet, they knew they had only enough ammunition left for one final volley against the attacking Indians.

While they watched and waited, all hope gone, the settlers suddenly felt drops of cool water on their heads. Rain was falling! Slowly the fires began to sputter and go out. All night and through the next day the rain continued, filling up the

wooden buckets. But because of a thick fog that had settled in the river valley, the settlers couldn't see what the Indians were doing. The eerie silence worried them. After a while, the tunnel guards heard digging and scraping noises coming from underground. Daniel listened, too. He heard the noise, but he couldn't tell how close the diggers were.

During the night the rain fell even harder while the settlers waited for the end, shivering in the damp cold. They were certain that at any moment the Indian diggers would reach the fort wall. Soon they would have to surrender.

Then morning came. The rain stopped. There was complete silence everywhere. Not even the sound of any digging. Suddenly one of the lookouts shouted that the Indians' tunnel had collapsed. He could see huge caved-in places filled with water.

To everyone's amazement, the Indians had left. They had given up for good. At last the settlers could fling open the gates and walk out of the fort. The Kentuckians had lost just two men; the Indians had lost at least thirty-seven.

But the small force at Boonesborough had done more than save their own fort. They had saved Kentucky for the new United States. And no man deserved more credit for the victory than Daniel Boone.

Bad Times in Kentucky

No one had worked harder to save Boonesborough than Daniel Boone. But many settlers didn't seem to appreciate what he had done. Instead they said he was guilty of treason. Colonel Callaway's nasty rumors began to find more and more friendly ears. Some accused him of being a British sympathizer. It was well known that Rebecca's family had remained loyal to England. Others thought that Boone must have made some sort of deal with Governor Hamilton. They suspected that he had plotted with the British to surrender the fort. William Hancock, the escaped salt worker, continued to tell his stories about the way Daniel had received friendly treatment by Chief Blackfish and the Shawnee.

Finally Colonel Callaway convinced Captain Logan, who was in charge of Logan's Station, to court-martial Daniel Boone. A court-martial is a military trial. Daniel was placed under arrest and taken to Logan's Station for the trial. Daniel couldn't believe what was happening. He had given his life to save Boonesborough, and now he was under arrest!

At the trial, Daniel was accused of many crimes, including treason, deliberately surrendering the salt workers to the enemy, and joining forces with the Indians. Since no witnesses came forward to help him, Daniel's future looked grim indeed.

Finally it was Daniel's turn to speak. In his usual quiet, sensible way, he explained exactly what he had done and why. He had never used tricks or told lies, he said, except to help his own people. And he did not support the British. He did not share the political beliefs of Rebecca's family. But he did uphold their right to believe as they wished. Daniel also pointed out that he didn't have to return to Boonesborough when he escaped from Chief Blackfish. He could have gone straight to North Carolina to join his family. Instead he risked his life to save the fort and its people. Would a traitor have risked his own life this way?

The members of the court saw that Daniel was telling the truth and found him innocent of any wrongdoing. In fact, they went even further. They raised his rank from captain to major, praising his bravery in saving the fort from destruction.

Because of the trial, Daniel had to wait until fall to join his family in North Carolina. Rebecca and the children had been living with her brother Samuel and his wife. At first Rebecca did not want to return to Kentucky. It took Daniel almost a year to persuade her to return to Boonesborough. When they finally left, several other relatives—including Daniel's brother Ned—went with them.

Since the victory at Boonesborough and another defeat of the Indians farther northwest, nearly twenty thousand settlers had made the trip to Kentucky. And all of them had traveled by way of the Wilderness Road. When the Boone caravan arrived at Boonesborough in October 1779, they found a settlement almost bursting with people. A school had been set up, and farmers were busy harvesting a huge corn crop. There was even talk of running a regular ferry across the Kentucky River.

As usual, when Daniel saw so many people crowded together, he wanted to get away. The family loaded their belongings onto packhorses and traveled northwest to a spot where Daniel had already established a land claim. He called it Boone's Station. There he built a log house and a small fort.

The new Virginia legislature ruled that all the land grants made by Henderson and the Transylvania Company were illegal. The state sent agents to Kentucky to sort out the settlers' claims. Daniel legally owned about three thousand acres.

He sold the land to raise money to buy a larger amount of land. In the spring he left for Richmond to secure legal papers for the purchase. Some other settlers gave him money to buy land for them. In all, he was carrying almost fifty thousand dollars in cash, hidden in his saddlebags.

One night Daniel and his traveling companion stopped at a Virginia inn. After dinner, they went to sleep. In the morning they discovered that someone had broken into their room and stolen all their money! Daniel challenged the innkeeper. He suspected he had been drugged. He wanted his money back. The innkeeper denied any part in the theft, and Daniel had no proof. The money was never found. Now he had no money and no way to buy more property. Worse yet, part of the stolen money belonged to his friends. He swore he would repay them, and eventually he did. But paying the money back kept him almost penniless for many years.

Meanwhile, the British armies had been successful in the south, and they were stirring up the Indian tribes again. During the summer of 1780, a British captain named Henry Bird marched into Kentucky with a force of seven hundred Indians. They destroyed many forts and killed large numbers of settlers. The terrifying news spread from one settlement to another. Settlers began to stream out of Kentucky almost as fast as they had poured in.

In the fall Daniel went off with his brother Ned to make salt. They spent several days at Blue Licks, then started home again. While they were resting in a small wooded area, they spotted a bear across the creek. Daniel quickly took a shot at it. Wounded, the bear staggered off. Daniel followed. Ned stayed behind. Suddenly Daniel heard shots. Then a Shawnee shouted, "It's Boone! We killed old Boone!" Daniel realized with horror that they had shot Ned. People had always said that the two brothers looked alike. The Indians must have thought they killed Daniel.

Before Daniel could return to Ned, an Indian dog picked up his scent and rushed toward him, growling. Daniel darted into a thick canebrake to escape. But the dog wouldn't go away. It kept barking as it chased Daniel through the thick woods. Finally Daniel had no choice but to shoot the dog. There was no other way to escape. As soon as it was safe, he went back to look for Ned. Once again, he had the sad job of burying a member of his own family.

Soon after this, Daniel was made a lieutenant colonel in the militia. In April 1781 he went to Richmond to represent the settlers in the Virginia Assembly. But by the spring of 1782 he was back in Kentucky fighting Indians again. In the East most of the fighting had finished. The French had joined the colonies in defeating England.

And General George Washington had beaten Lord Cornwallis at Yorktown, Virginia. The colonies had won the revolution.

The British had not given up the territory west of the Appalachian Mountains. Their Indian allies were still attacking settlements. In August, Daniel was part of a group of militiamen heading toward the Licking River. There were about 180 riflemen under the general command of Lieutenant Colonel John Todd. Daniel was in charge of all the men from his county. His son Israel, and some other relatives, were part of his group.

Three hundred Wyandot Indians and fifty British soldiers had just raided Bryan's Station, a few miles from Boonesborough, where they had burned all the crops and killed about six hundred cattle, sheep, and hogs. The militiamen were looking for them.

When the Kentuckians reached the Licking River, there were no Indians in sight. Clearly they must have crossed the river already. The angry militiamen wanted to chase them immediately. But Daniel thought they should be more cautious. He knew the area well. It would be very easy for the Indians to hide here.

The group took a vote and Daniel lost. Colonel Todd gave the order to cross the river. He felt he had enough men to handle a surprise Indian attack. The men crossed the river on horseback. Then they walked up the hill on foot. When they looked down from the hilltop, they couldn't see a single Indian. As the Kentuckians started walking down the other side of the hill, the Indian warriors let loose with a horrifying blast of gunfire. The Indians had hidden in ditches covered by brush. How could the settlers fight an enemy they couldn't see? The battle turned into a bloody massacre.

Daniel fought as long as he could, but in the end he too was forced to retreat, just ahead of his son Israel. Daniel headed toward a creek he knew well. Suddenly, from behind, he heard a shotgun blast. Daniel turned just in time to see his son fall to the ground. A bullet had caught him right in the chest. With gunfire blasting all around him, Daniel rushed back and picked Israel up in his arms. He carried him through the woods and over a creek to a cave he knew. There he lay his son down gently. There was nothing he could do. His son was dead. He started back to Boone's Station to give Rebecca the tragic news.

When it was safe, he returned to the cave and brought Israel's body back to Boone's Station to be buried. The twenty-three-year-old boy had died in the last major battle of the Revolutionary War.

The Last Move

On a clear September day in 1799, a large group of people gathered on the shore of the Ohio River. They had come to say a final good-bye to Daniel and Rebecca Boone. The Boones and many of their relatives and friends were moving to Missouri. Daniel had cut down a tall yellow poplar tree to make a giant sixty-foot canoe. It was big enough to hold the family's possessions and supplies, as well as the women and children. Daniel's sons Daniel Morgan and Nathan and his brother Squire were in charge of the fleet of boats that were traveling together. Daniel and two of his sons-in-law were making the trip by land, walking all seven hundred miles. They were taking a herd of cattle and horses with them.

Seventeen years had passed since Israel's death at Licking River. Those seventeen years had brought bad luck to Daniel. He had tried growing tobacco at Boone's Station, and he and Rebecca had run a tavern on the banks of the Ohio River. They also lived for a while in West Virginia. But nothing seemed to work out.

For several years Daniel worked as a surveyor, finding good land and marking it off for new arrivals. Kentucky had become a state in 1792, and six years later there were at least seventy-five thousand settlers living there. Daniel knew where to find the best land, and he was not afraid to go into dangerous territory in search of it.

Many of the new settlers could not afford to pay him in cash. Instead they gave him some of the land they were claiming. Slowly Daniel put together a fortune in land—at least a hundred thousand acres in claims.

Unfortunately, Daniel was never very interested in the details of filing claims. And settlers were not very precise about marking off boundaries. There were constant court battles over who owned what. Many of the settlers who had built cabins, cut down trees, and plowed fields suddenly found that for one reason or another their claims were not legal. They were forced to leave the property they had worked so hard to prepare for crops. Settlers who had paid Daniel to survey their lands now sued him for having failed to record the claims properly.

There were also many land speculators who cheated honest owners out of their property. Some of these speculators had cheated Daniel out of his land. By the time Daniel finished paying off all the people who claimed he owed them money, he had almost nothing left for himself. He was no longer happy in Kentucky. It was becoming too crowded, and there was little game to hunt. He was ready to explore new places.

The opportunity came when Daniel Morgan Boone returned from a trip to Missouri. He told his father that the Spanish government, which now owned the Missouri territory, had offered Daniel 850 acres of land if he would lead a group of settlers there. They had offered smaller land grants to all the families that Daniel brought with him. Daniel Morgan told his father that very few people lived in Missouri, and the land was filled with game.

Although Daniel was now sixty-four years old, he eagerly decided to make the move to Missouri. He was ready to leave Kentucky with all its heartaches and disappointments. He didn't realize how popular he was, however, until he saw the crowd that turned out to say farewell. Some people came simply because they had heard so many stories about the legendary frontiersman. They were curious to see what he looked like.

Almost a year passed before the Boones arrived at St. Louis. The Spanish were delighted to have the famous explorer there, and they greeted him with ceremony and honors. Daniel picked out 850 acres of rich land for himself about sixty miles west of St. Louis. It was next to Daniel Morgan's property. The family set up a maple sugar camp, and Daniel built a log cabin on his son's land.

In 1800, the Spanish appointed Daniel *syndic* of his region. This job combined the duties of sheriff, judge, and jury in one person. Daniel did not believe in trials and other legal procedures. He had suffered too much at the hands of lawyers and judges. What interested him was the truth. He held his court outdoors under a big elm he called the Judgment Tree. There he settled arguments in a sensible manner. He was very fair, and explained things in a way people could understand. Later, when a new government did away with the job of syndic, people still came to Daniel, asking him to settle their disputes.

Even though he was the syndic, Daniel had plenty of time to hunt and trap. In just one spring he sold more than nine hundred beaver skins. Also, the Spanish governor soon realized that people were coming to Missouri because of Daniel Boone. To express his appreciation, he increased Daniel's land grant to 8,500 acres.

In 1803, the territory known as Missouri changed owners again. Spain was forced to give the land back to France. The French emperor Napoleon needed money, so he sold more than eight hundred thousand square miles to the United States. This sale was called the Louisiana

Purchase. It doubled the size of the new country, which now stretched west to the Rocky Mountains and south to the Gulf of Mexico.

The new purchase brought more troubles for Daniel. The American government refused to recognize his land claim, partly because he had never built a house or planted a crop on it. This was an enormous disappointment to Daniel, who had always longed to own a great deal of land. Later, a special act of Congress granted Daniel 850 acres to make up for his loss. But he soon had to give up that to repay old debts.

In 1812, war broke out again between Britain and the United States. Daniel was seventy-eight years old. Still, he tried to join the American army. He was insulted when they told him he was too old for active duty.

The next year, Rebecca was boiling maple-sugar sap in the woods. She suddenly felt sick and the next day she died. Her death was a terrible blow to Daniel. Although he had spent long periods of time away from her and the children, he had come to depend very much on her loyalty and courage. It was difficult to imagine a life without her.

Though Daniel's hair was now snow-white, his eyes were still the same brilliant, piercing blue. He continued to hunt and explore. On his last long trip he followed the Platte River all the way to the Rockies. There he spent the winter trapping in the Yellowstone country. He had never seen anything to match the steaming geysers and the tall craggy mountains that surrounded him. He had traveled six hundred miles—remarkable for a man who was eighty years old.

One day, after his return to Missouri, an artist came from St. Louis to paint a portrait of Daniel. The artist's name was Chester Harding. Harding later reported that he asked the old man if in all his travels he had ever been lost. Daniel replied, "No, I can't say as ever I was lost, but I was once bewildered for three days." Old friends of Daniel's suspected that there must have been the twitch of a smile on his face when the old man gave his answer.

Daniel never liked the portrait. He thought his cheeks looked too sunken in and his lips too tightly drawn around the gums. It was the only portrait of him done from life. The famous bird artist John James Audubon once encountered Daniel during a trek through the wilderness. Apparently the two men took to each other right away. They shared a mutual love of nature. While they were together, Audubon made a few sketches of Daniel's face.

For his last expedition Daniel planned to travel on foot all the way to California. He never made it. During the summer of 1820 he was taken with a fever at his daughter Jemima's house. He refused to give in to it, getting out of bed to ride over to his son Nathan's house. After eating some sweet potatoes, he began to feel sick again, so he went to bed in the corner bedroom that was kept especially for him. And there, on September 26, he died in his sleep.

In St. Louis a group of men were meeting to draft a constitution for Missouri, which was soon to become a state. When the group heard that Daniel had died, they immediately ended their meeting. For twenty days they wore black bands on their coat sleeves—one day for each year that Daniel had lived in Missouri.

Daniel was buried next to Rebecca in a graveyard that overlooked some fine acres of Missouri land.

In 1845, the people of Missouri agreed to have the remains of Daniel and Rebecca removed to Frankfort, the state capital of Kentucky. The Kentuckians wanted to have the famous pioneer brought home to the state that owed its very existence to Daniel Boone.

Epilogue

In 1784, a man from Kentucky named John Filson wrote a book called *The Discovery, Settlement and Present State of Kentucke*. At the end of the book he added a thirty-four-page appendix. Filson called this appendix an "autobiography" of Daniel Boone. Filson claimed that he had many conversations with Daniel Boone. He also claimed that Daniel Boone himself had approved the article. Today historians doubt that Daniel Boone ever had anything to do with the article. But when the book was published, people loved reading about the colorful adventures of this hunter, explorer, and Indian fighter.

Unfortunately, Daniel Boone never wrote an autobiography. While living in Missouri, he started telling the story of his life to one of Jemima's sons. During the War of 1812, however, Jemima and the rest of the Callaway family had to flee from their farm. Jemima's husband, Flanders Callaway, packed the family possessions in a canoe and started down the Missouri River. Before he had gone far, the canoe hit a rock and sank. Callaway swam to safety, but the family possessions disappeared forever. The precious manuscript of Daniel Boone's life was lost.

Many other books about Daniel Boone were written, but these books contained stories that were not true. James Fenimore Cooper, an early American writer, based the hero of *The Deerslayer* —one of the novels in the famous *Leatherstocking Tales*—on Daniel. But the real Daniel Boone disappeared for many years in a cloud of myth.

Daniel Boone would never have wanted to be remembered as an Indian fighter. Born into the Quaker religion, he was basically a peaceful man. He loved the wilderness and respected the traditions and woodland knowledge of the native Americans. But since he knew so much about the Indians, he knew how to fight them. When the Indians attacked, he saved many settlers' lives and many a fort.

What Daniel Boone *should* be remembered for is the important part he played in the opening and settling of the West. He was one of the first white Americans to cross the Appalachian Mountains and explore the fabulously rich territory of Kentucky and the Ohio Valley region. Daniel Boone and his road cutters blazed a trail across the mountains—the Wilderness Road—that thousands of pioneers used for their journey west.

By bringing his own family to Kentucky, Daniel Boone gave others the courage to settle there. And he played a big part in defending the land against both the Indians and the British. But most important, Daniel Boone was the kind of man who always wanted to know what he would find across the next river, what he would see if he climbed the next mountain. He forever hated to be cooped in. He loved exploring the unknown and revealing it to others.

Without Daniel Boone and other frontiersmen like him, the United States might still be huddled along the shores of the Atlantic Ocean.

Highlights in the Life of
DANIEL BOONE

1734   Daniel Boone is born on November 2 in Berks County, Pennsylvania.

1747   Daniel kills his first bear.

1750   Daniel and his family begin the long trip to North Carolina.

1754   The French and Indian War breaks out.

1755   Daniel serves under General Braddock in the campaign to drive the French from Fort Duquesne. John Findley tells Daniel about the wonders of the Kentucky territory.

1756   Daniel marries Rebecca Bryan.

1758   Daniel serves under General John Forbes in a successful attack against Fort Duquesne.

1763   The French and Indian War officially ends, with Britain gaining control of eastern North America. England forbids colonists to settle west of the Appalachian Mountains.

1765 Daniel and some friends explore Florida.

1767 Daniel reaches Kentucky for the first time.

1769 Daniel, John Findley, and four others set off to explore Kentucky.

1770 British soldiers kill five colonists in the Boston Massacre.

1773 On September 26, Daniel sets out for Kentucky with his family. Indians attack them and kill his son James.

Americans dressed like Indians creep onto British ships and dump their tea cargo into Boston Harbor.

1775 In March, Daniel and his road cutters finish the Wilderness Road and establish the settlement of Boonesborough.

In April, the Revolutionary War begins at Lexington and Concord, Massachusetts.

In September, Daniel brings his family and a party of settlers to Boonesborough.

1776	The Declaration of Independence is signed on July 4. Less than two weeks later, Indians kidnap Jemima Boone and her two friends.
1777	Chief Blackfish leads an unsuccessful Shawnee attack against Fort Boonesborough.
1778	Shawnee warriors capture Daniel and the salt workers at Lower Blue Licks in February. Shawnee attack Fort Boonesborough in September. Daniel is court-martialed and found innocent.
1779	Twenty thousand settlers flock to Kentucky.
1780	British defeat Americans in North Carolina.
1781	Americans defeat British at Yorktown, Virginia. Daniel represents Kentucky in the Virginia Assembly.
1782	Wyandot Indians and British defeat Kentuckians at Licking Run.
1783	Great Britain officially recognizes the independent United States.
1789	George Washington is elected first president.

1792   Kentucky becomes the fifteenth state.

1799   Daniel leads settlers to Missouri.
George Washington dies.

1800   Daniel is appointed *syndic* in Missouri.

1803   The United States purchases the Louisiana Territory from France, nearly doubling the size of the country.

1812   War breaks out between the United States and Great Britain.

1813   Rebecca Boone dies on March 18.

1815   Daniel travels to the Rockies and the Yellowstone country.

1820   Daniel Boone dies on September 26.

	DATE DUE		